Practical Pre-School
Planning for Learning through Food

by Rachel Sparks Linfield   Illustrated by Cathy Hughes

Contents

Published by Step Forward Publishing Limited
St Jude's Church, Dulwich Road, Herne Hill, London, SE24 0PB Tel. 020 7738 5454
Revised edition © Step Forward Publishing Limited 2008
First edition © Step Forward Publishing Limited 2001
www.practicalpreschool.com
Planning for Learning through Food ISBN: 978 1 90457 577 1

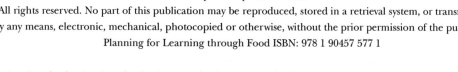

Making plans

Why plan?

The purpose of planning is to make sure that all children enjoy a broad and balanced curriculum. All planning should be useful. Plans are working documents that you spend time preparing, but which should later repay your efforts. Try to be concise. This will help you in finding information quickly when you need it.

Long-term plans

Preparing a long-term plan, which maps out the curriculum during a year or even two, will help you to ensure that you are providing a variety of activities and are meeting the statutory requirements of the Statutory Framework for the Early Years Foundation Stage (2007).

Your long-term plan need not be detailed. Divide the time period over which you are planning into fairly equal sections, such as half terms. Choose a topic for each section. Young children benefit from making links between the new ideas they encounter so as you select each topic, think about the time of year in which you plan to do it. A topic about minibeasts will not be very successful in November!

Although each topic will address all the learning areas, some could focus on a specific area. For example, a topic on Food would lend itself well to activities relating to Personal, Social and Emotional Development, Creative Development and Knowledge and Understanding of the

World. Another topic might particularly encourage the appreciation of stories. Try to make sure that you provide a variety of topics in your long-term plans.

Autumn 1	Nursery rhymes
Autumn 2	Food/Christmas
Spring 1	People who help us
Spring 2	Weath
Summer 1	Clothes
Summer 2	Minibeasts

Medium-term plans

Medium-term plans will outline the contents of a topic in a little more detail. One way to start this process is by brainstorming on a large piece of paper. Work with your team writing down all the activities you can think of which are relevant to the topic. As you do this it may become clear that some activities go well together. Think about dividing them into themes. The topic of Food, for example, has themes such as 'Favourite food', 'Buying and selling food', 'Fruit and vegetables', 'Food from around the world', 'Food from fairy tales and nursery rhymes' and 'Food for special occasions'. At this stage it is helpful to make a chart. Write the theme ideas down the side of the chart and put a different area of learning at the top of each column. Now you can insert your brainstormed ideas and will quickly see where there are gaps. As you complete the chart take account of children's earlier experiences and provide opportunities for them to progress.

Refer back to Statutory Framework for the Early Years Foundation Stage and check that you have addressed as many different aspects of it as you can. Once all your medium-term plans are complete make sure that there are no neglected areas.

Day-to-day plans

The plans you make for each day will outline aspects such as:

● resources needed;
● individual needs;

Making plans

- safety;
- the way in which you might introduce activities;
- the organisation of adult help;
- size of the group;
- timing;
- key vocabulary.

Identify the learning and the ELGs that each activity intends to promote. Make a note of any assessments or observations that you are likely to carry out. Aftercarrying out the activitites make notes on your plans to say what was particularly successful, or any changes you would make another time.

A final note

Planning should be seen as flexible. Not all groups meet every day, and not all children attend every day. Any part of the plan can be used independently, stretched over a longer period or condensed to meet the needs of any group. You will almost certainly adapt the activities as children respond to them in different ways and bring their own ideas, interests and enthusiasms. The important thing is to ensure that the children are provided with a varied and enjoyable curriculum that meets their individual developing needs.

Using the book

- Collect or prepare suggested resources as listed on page 21.
- Read the section which outlines links to the Early Learning Goals (pages 4-7) and explains the rationale for the topic of Food.
- For each weekly theme two activities are described in detail as an example to help you in your planning and preparation. Key vocabulary, questions and learning opportunities are identified.
- The skills chart on page 23 will help you to see at a glance which aspects of children's development are being addressed as a focus each week.
- As children take part in the Food topic activities, their learning will progress.

'Collecting evidence' on page 22 explains how you might monitor children's achievements.
- Find out on page 20 how the topic can be brought together in a grand finale involving parents, children and friends.
- There is additional material to support the working partnership of families and children in the form of a 'Home links' page, and a photocopiable 'Parent's page' found at the back of the book.

It is important to appreciate that the ideas presented in this book will only be a part of your planning. Many activities that will be taking place as routine in your group may not be mentioned. For example, it is assumed that sand, dough, water, puzzles, floor toys and large scale apparatus are part of the ongoing pre-school experience, as are the opportunities to develop ICT skills. Role-play areas, stories, rhymes and singing, and group discussion times are similarly assumed to be happening each week although they may not be a focus for described activities. Groups should also ensure that there is a balance of adult-led and child-initiated activities.

When planning the Food topic remember to check children's health records for food allergies/food they may not eat. Ensure that parents are aware of the planned themes. Do not attempt any baking or tasting activity without parental consent and remember to consult your area health and safety guidelines.

Using the 'Early Learning Goals'

Having chosen your topic and made your medium-term plans you can use the document Early Learning Goals to highlight the key learning opportunities your activities will address. The Early Learning Goals are split into six areas: Personal, Social and Emotional Development; Communication, Language and Literacy; Problem Solving, Reasoning and Numeracy; Knowledge and Understanding of the World; Physical Development and Creative Development. Do not expect each of your topics to cover every goal but your long-term plans should allow for all of them to be addressed by the time a child enters Year 1.

The following section lists the ELGs in point form to show what children are expected to be able to do in each area of learning by the time they enter Year 1. These points will be used throughout this book to show how activities for a topic on Food link to these expectations. For example, Personal, Social and Emotional Development point 7 is 'form good relationships with peers and adults'. Activities suggested which provide the opportunity for children to do this will have the reference PS7. This will enable you to see which parts of the Early Learning Goals are covered in a given week and plan for areas to be revisited and developed.

In addition, you can ensure that activities offer variety in the goals to be encountered. Often a similar activity may be carried out to achieve different learning objectives. For example, during this topic children join in a number rhyme about eating grapes. Children will be developing areas of Problem Solving, Reasoning and Numeracy as they count grapes. They will also be using personal and social skills as they choose friends to pick grapes and collaborate to recite and mime the rhyme. It is important, therefore, that activities have clearly defined goals so that these may be emphasised during the activity and for recording purposes.

Personal, Social and Emotional Development (PS)

This area of learning covers important aspects of development that affect the way children learn, behave and relate to others.

By the end of the EYFS children should:

PS1   Continue to be interested, excited and motivated to learn.

PS2   Be confident to try new activities, initiate ideas and speak in a familiar group.

PS3   Maintain attention, concentrate, and sit quietly when appropriate.

PS4   Respond to significant experiences, showing a range of feelings when appropriate.

PS5   Have a developing awareness of their own needs, views and feelings, and be sensitive to the needs, views and feelings of others.

PS6   Have a developing respect for their own cultures and beliefs and those of other people.

PS7   Form good relationships with peers and adults.

PS8   Work as part of a group or class taking turns and sharing fairly; understanding that there need to be agreed values and codes of behaviour for groups of people, including adults and children, to work harmoniously.

PS9   Understand what is right, what is wrong and why.

PS10   Consider the consequences of their words and actions for themselves and others.

PS11   Dress and undress independently and manage their own personal hygiene.

PS12   Select and use activities and resources independently.

PS13   Understand that people have different needs, views, cultures and beliefs that need to be treated with respect.

PS14   Understand that they can expect others to treat their needs, views, cultures and beliefs with respect.

The topic of Food offers many opportunities for children's personal, social and emotional development. Time spent discussing favourite foods will encourage children to speak in a group, to be interested and to consider consequences. By playing circle games children will learn to take turns and to understand the need for agreed codes of behaviour. Many of the areas outlined above, though, will be covered on an almost incidental basis as children carry out the activities described in this book for the other areas of learning. During undirected free choice times they will be developing PS12 whilst any small group activity that involves working with an adult will help children to work towards PS7.

Communication, Language and Literacy (L)

By the end of the EYFS children should:

L1   Interact with others, negotiating plans and activities and taking turns in conversation.

L2   Enjoy listening to and using spoken and written language, and readily turn to it in their play and learning.

L3   Sustain attentive listening, responding to what they have heard with relevant comments, questions or actions.

L4   Listen with enjoyment and respond to stories, songs and other music, rhymes and poems and make up their own stories, songs, rhymes and poems.

L5   Extend their vocabulary, exploring the meanings and sounds of new words.

L6   Speak clearly and audibly with confidence and control and show awareness of the listener.

L7   Use language to imagine and recreate roles and experiences .

L8   Use talk to organise, sequence and clarify thinking, ideas, feelings and events.

L9   Hear and say sounds in words in the order in which they occur.

L10   Link sounds to letters, naming and sounding the letters of the alphabet.

L11   Use their phonic knowledge to write simple regular words and make phonetically plausible attempts at more complex words.

L12   Explore and experiment with sounds, words and texts.

L13   Retell narratives in the correct sequence, drawing on language patterns of stories.

L14   Read a range of familiar and common words and simple sentences independently.

L15   Know that print carries meaning and, in English, is read from left to right and top to bottom.

L16   Show an understanding of the elements of stories, such as main character, sequence of events and openings and how information can be found in non-fiction texts to answer questions about where, who, why and how.

L17   Attempt writing for various purposes, using features of different forms such as lists, stories and instructions.

L18   Write their own names and other things such as labels and captions, and begin to form simple sentences, sometimes using punctuation.

L19   Use a pencil and hold it effectively to form recognisable letters, most of which are correctly formed.

There is a wide range of quality fiction and non-fiction books which feature food. A number of the activities suggested for the theme of Food are based on well-known picture books and stories. They allow children to enjoy listening to the books and to respond in a variety of ways to what they hear, reinforcing and extending their vocabularies. Throughout the topic opportunities are described in which children are encouraged to use descriptive vocabulary and to see some of their ideas recorded in both pictures and words. Role-play areas are described that will allow children to use their

imagination as they sell food on a market stall, work in a travel agency or are customers at a cafe.

Problem Solving, Reasoning and Numeracy (N)

By the end of the EYFS children should:

N1   Say and use number names in order in familiar contexts.

N2   Count reliably up to ten everyday objects.

N3   Recognise numerals 1 to 9.

N4   use developing mathematical ideas and methods to solve practical problems.

N5   In practical activities and discussion, begin to use the vocabulary involved in adding and subtracting.

N6   Use language such as 'more' or 'less' to compare two numbers.

N7   Find one more or one less than a number from one to ten.

N8   Begin to relate addition to combining two groups of objects and subtraction to 'taking away'.

N9   Use language such as 'greater', 'smaller', heavier' or 'lighter' to compare quantities.

N10 Talk about, recognise and recreate simple patterns.

N11 Use language such as 'circle' or 'bigger' to describe the shape and size of solids and flat shapes.

N12 Use everyday words to describe position

The theme of Food provides a meaningful context for mathematical activities. As children play number games based on food they are encouraged to count, to recognise numbers and to begin to develop language for addition and subtraction. Pasta and long vegetables are used as non-standard units for measuring. There are opportunities for children to explore shape, size and position as children make collages of food using regular shapes.

Knowledge and Understanding of the World (K)

By the end of the EYFS children should:

K1   Investigate objects and materials by using all of their senses as appropriate.

K2   Find out about, and identify, some features of living things, objects and events they observe.

K3   Look closely at similarities, differences, patterns and change.

K4   Ask questions about why things happen and how things work.

K5   Build and construct with a wide range of objects, selecting appropriate resources and adapting their work where necessary.

K6   Select the tools and techniques they need to shape, assemble and join materials they are using.

K7   Find out about and identify the uses of everyday technology and use information and communication technology and programmable toys to support their learning.

K8   Find out about past and present events in their own lives, and in those of their families and other people they know.

K9   Observe, find out about and identify features in the place they live and the natural world.

K10   Find out about their environment, and talk about those features they like and dislike.

K11   Begin to know about their own cultures and beliefs and those of other people.

The Food theme offers opportunities for children to make observations, to ask questions and to compare. They can observe a range of fruit and vegetables. By looking at and talking about food from around the world and food for special occasions they will become aware of the wide variety in types of food. Activities such as making salt dough, fruit salad and biscuits will give children the opportunity to describe materials and to talk about similarities, differences and changes.

Physical Development (PD)

By the end of the EYFS children should:

PD1   Move with confidence, imagination and in safety.

PD2   Move with control and coordination.

PD3   Travel around, under, over and through balancing and climbing equipment.

PD4   Show awareness of space, of themselves and of others.

PD5   Recognise the importance of keeping healthy and those things which contribute to this.

PD6   Recognise the changes that happen to their bodies when they are active.

PD7   Use a range of small and large equipment

PD8   Handle tools, objects, construction and malleable materials safely and with increasing control.

Activities such as playing with modelling dough will offer experience of PD8. Through pretending to be seeds and miming going to market children will have the opportunity to move with control and imagination and develop awareness of safety and space. Through using a range of small and large equipment as they pretend to buy and sell food and pick fruit they will be encouraged to develop their coordination and control.

Creative Development (C)

By the end of the EYFS children should:

C1   Respond in a variety of ways to what they see, hear, smell, touch and feel.

C2   Express and communicate their ideas, thoughts and feelings by using a widening range of materials, suitable tools, imaginative and role-play, movement, designing and making, and a variety of songs and musical instruments.

C3   Explore colour, texture, shape, form and space in two or three dimensions.

C4   Recognise and explore how sounds can be changed, sing simple songs from memory, recognise repeated sounds and sound patterns and match movements to music.

C5   Use their imagination in art and design, music, dance, imaginative and role play and stories.

During this topic children will experience working with a variety of materials as they make collages of favourite meals. They will be able to develop their skills of painting and colour mixing as they paint portraits of fairy tale and nursery rhyme characters and food and so work towards C3 and C5. A number of songs have been suggested which could also have actions and percussion added, so allowing children to use their imagination in music. Throughout all the activities children are encouraged to talk about what they see and feel as they communicate their ideas in painting, collage work and role play.

Week 1
Favourite food

Personal, Social and Emotional Development

- During a circle time talk about favourite food. (PS2, 3)
- Look at a picture of a country hit by a famine. Discuss the importance of sharing. (PS4)
- During snack time provide a selection of healthy drinks. Invite children to choose their favourite and explain why. (PS4)

Communication, Language and Literacy

- Invite children to make menus for a favourite meal. (L17)
- Read the story of Paddington Bear's arrival in London found in *A Bear Called Paddington* by Michael Bond (Harper Collins). Talk about Paddington's favourite marmalade sandwiches. On triangles of paper ask children to make new sandwiches for Paddington (see activity opposite). (L3)
- Begin a collection of words to describe favourite foods. Collect the words in a sandwich box. (L11, 14)

Problem Solving, Reasoning and Numeracy

- Make a group number line with pictures of favourite foods. Encourage children to recognise numbers to ten. (N1, 2, 3)
- Provide each child with a paper plate holding ten pictures of favourite foods. Play a game in which children in turn throw a die and 'eat' the corresponding number of foods. After each turn encourage children to say how many foods remain on their plates. The winner is the one who has the first empty plate. (N1, 2, 5)
- Use brown paper triangles and coloured circles to make collages of ice-cream cones (see activity opposite). (N11)

Knowledge and Understanding of the World

- Look through books about animals to identify favourite foods for animals. Encourage children to draw picture menus of favourite foods for a minibeast. (K2)
- Use clean packaging from favourite foods to build large models such as castles, vehicles, dinosaurs and robots. Show children how to cover plastic containers with masking tape before attempting to paint them and how to undo and remake, inside out, cereal packets to provide clean surfaces to decorate. (K5)

Physical Development

- Use dough and paper plates to make models of favourite food. (PD8)
- Encourage children to work in pairs as they aim small foam balls to be caught in cones made from card. Pretend the balls are ice cream which needs to be caught before it melts. (PD8)

Creative Development

- Paint pictures of favourite food. Encourage children to think carefully about shapes and colours. (C3)
- In the home corner encourage children to prepare favourite meals for their friends. (C5)
- Make favourite food posters by cutting pictures from magazines and wrapping paper. Encourage children to describe the way the food looks and tastes. (C1)

Activity: Favourite Sandwiches

Learning opportunity: Responding to stories and identifying initial sounds.

Early Learning Goal: Communication, Language and Literacy. Children should sustain attentive listening, responding to what they have heard with relevant comments, questions or actions.

Resources: *A Bear Called Paddington* by Michael Bond (Harper Collins); squares of brown and white paper of side length 21cm; crayons; pencils.

Key vocabulary: Sandwich, names for fillings, favourite.

Organisation: Whole group for the story, small group for making sandwiches.

What to do: Read the story of Paddington's arrival in England. Talk about his favourite sandwiches being ones filled with marmalade. Show children a square of paper and how to fold it diagonally to make two triangles. Inside colour it orange to represent marmalade. Ask children to say which sound the word 'marmalade' begins with. Write an 'm' on the front of the sandwich. Invite a small group to come and make paper sandwiches filled with their favourite fillings. Help children to write the initial sounds for the fillings. When all the sandwiches have been made use them to play a game of 'Guess what is inside this sandwich. It is something beginning with ...'.

Activity: Making ice-cream cornets

Learning opportunity: Talking about flat shapes.

Early Learning Goal: Problem Solving, Reasoning and Numeracy. Children will be able to use language such as 'circle' or 'bigger' to describe the shape and size of solids and flat shapes.

Resources: Triangles to represent ice-cream cones cut from brown paper; circles to represent ice cream cut from a variety of pastel shades of paper; scraps for adding decoration to the ice cream; crayons.

Key vocabulary: Triangle, circle, ice cream.

Organisation: Small group.

What to do: Tell the group that some people's favourite food is ice cream. Talk about different ice creams that the group has eaten and which flavours they like best. Show how to stick coloured circles onto a piece of paper in a clump with a triangle underneath to make a picture of an ice-cream cornet. Add a small brown rectangle for a chocolate flake. Invite children to make their own ice creams. Encourage them to use the names for the shapes and to talk about their ice creams' flavours.

Display

In the centre of a large board write 'My favourite food is ...'. At the bottom of the board put up the group's favourite food number line. At the top of the board arrange the ice-cream cones with labels of the flavours. Cover a table with a bright tablecloth and place it in front of the board. Put out the paper sandwiches on plastic plates, the dough food and also the sandwich box word collections.

Week 2
Buying and selling food

Personal, Social and Emotional Development

- During a circle time mime buying and selling food. Talk about the need to say 'please' and 'thank you' and how it feels to be thanked. (PS8, 9)
- Encourage children to say 'please' and 'thank-you' when they participate in a role-play cafe, shop or market stall. (PS8, 9)

Communication, Language and Literacy

- Play 'I went to the market'. Encourage children in turn to suggest a food that has been bought and to remember to say all the items that others have bought. (L2)
- Help children to make name signs for cafes. Encourage them to use their own names in the signs. Each day, display a different one in a role-play cafe area. (L18)
- Encourage children to be customers or waiters in the role-play cafe, to 'read' menus and to 'write' orders and bills. (L2, 17)

Problem Solving, Reasoning and Numeracy

- Enjoy buying and selling food in a role-play cafe. Make the price of food either one, two or ten pence. Provide real money for children to use. Encourage children to check that all the money is still present at the end of each session. (N1, 4, 5)
- Make a collection of boxes used to package biscuits and cereals. Use the boxes for sorting and building activities. (N11)
- Provide children with toy food and small baskets to buy a given number of food items (see activity opposite). (N1, 2, 3)

Knowledge and Understanding of the World

- Invite people known to the group who sell food to come and talk about their jobs. Before the talks encourage children to think of questions they would like to ask. Take photos and involve children in making a big book to record the visits. (K9)
- Investigate bar codes (see activity opposite). (K7)

- Make a collection of clean food packaging. Encourage children to sort them according to the materials from which they are made and the food that they contained. (K3)

Physical Development
- Make skittles by decorating empty plastic bottles with stickers. Play a game in which children 'buy' bottles by rolling a ball to knock the bottle over. Give the bottles prices of one or two pence. The winner is the child who 'spends' the most money. (PD6)
- Use coloured balls as pretend fruits. Encourage children to sort the fruits for selling at a market by throwing them into matching coloured baskets. (PD7)

Creative Development
- Use the menus made in Week 1 in a role-play cafe. Encourage children to enjoy taking orders, serving food and being customers. Provide receipt books for children to take orders and give bills. (C5)
- Make a collection of packets for cereals. Together look at the pictures on the boxes and talk about what the cereals might taste like. Help children to design and paint new pictures for cereal packets. Use the boxes in a role-play shop. (C2, 3, 5)
- Make purses from rectangles of felt with punched holes for the seams. Show children how to oversew using plastic needles and wool or embroidery silk. When finished make a fastening with sticky Velcro. Line the purse with a small envelope to make sure the money is safe! (C3)

Activity: Filling a basket

Learning opportunity: Counting to ten.

Early Learning Goal: Problem Solving, Reasoning and Numeracy. Children should say and use number names in order in familiar contexts. They should count reliably up to ten everyday objects. They should recognise numerals one to nine.

Resources: Selection of food cut from sugar paper; four small baskets; lists showing pictures of four of the sugar-paper foods and numbers from one to nine.

Key vocabulary: Numbers to nine, names of foods, list, buying.

Organisation: Small group.

What to do: Show children the sugar-paper foods and ask them to identify the foods. Show children a list and explain that shopping lists help people to remember what they want to buy when they go shopping. Together count out the foods to put in a basket. Give each child a different list and a basket. Encourage them to count out the correct number of foods for their basket. As a group check the baskets' contents. Finally provide blank lists for children to enjoy drawing their own foods for friends to buy.

Activity: Investigating bar codes

Learning opportunity: Observing and making patterns.

Early Learning Goal: Knowledge and Understanding of the World. Children should find out about and identify the uses of everyday technology...

Resources: Plastic magnifiers; packaging from foods with bar codes; sticky notes; thick and thin black washable felt pens; A4 paper; toy foods/packets for role-play foods.

Key vocabulary: Straight line, black, ruler, bar code, price, cost, how much.

Organisation: Small group.

What to do: Talk about visits to shops and the way that cashiers use bar codes to price foods. Explain that each type of food has a different bar code and that the code also gives the food's price. Together use magnifiers to examine bar codes. Encourage children to notice the way the patterns are made up of straight lines that vary in thickness and position.

Provide each child with sticky notes and a thick and a thin black felt pen. Show them how to make their own bar codes for toy foods. Encourage them to stick a note on each food and to copy their pattern onto a larger piece of paper alongside a picture of the food. Use the children's bar codes for role-play and matching activities.

Display
Cover a small board with black paper. Display children's bar codes along with a picture and word label to show what each code represents. Cover a second board with wallpaper. Use brown sugar paper and border strips to create the effect of shelves. Display children's designs for cereal packets on the shelves.

Week 3
Fruit and vegetables

Personal, Social and Emotional Development

- During a circle time enjoy sharing an apple. Talk about the taste and save the pips. (PS2, 3)
- Read Oliver's Fruit Salad by Vivian French (Hodder Children's Books). Mime making a fruit salad starting with the washing of hands and fruit. Talk about why it is important to wash hands. (PS9, 11)
- Encourage children to collaborate in using a role-play fruit and vegetable stall. Use papier mache fruit and vegetables made by the children (see Creative Development). Talk about the need to handle the fruit and vegetables with care. (PS9, 10)

Communication, Language and Literacy

- As a group, retell the story of Oliver's Fruit Salad. Make a list of all the fruits used in the book. Use the list to buy fruit and make a fruit salad to share. Lemonade makes an excellent syrup. (L4, 17)
- Read The Very Hungry Caterpillar by Eric Carle (Puffin). Involve the children in writing a new version in which the caterpillar eats vegetables (see activity opposite). (L4, 13)
- Invite children to take it in turn to describe a fruit or vegetable for the rest of the group to identify. Encourage children to be specific about colours, shapes, textures and sizes. (L2, 3, 8)

Problem Solving, Reasoning and Numeracy

- Enjoy using the grape rhyme (see activity opposite). (N1)
- Provide each child with a bunch of grapes made by drawing around a two pence coin ten times. Lay a green counter on each circle. Play a game in which children in turn throw a die and remove the corresponding number of grapes from their bunch. (N1, 2, 5)
- Use long vegetables such as carrots and beans for measuring lengths. (N9)

Knowledge and Understanding of the World

- Sort a basket of food into fruit and vegetables. Explain that fruits are foods that contain seeds. Introduce tomatoes as fruits. (Note: Strawberries are an exception to this definition of a fruit as they have seeds on the outside!) (K3)
- Having first gained permission from children's carers, enjoy tasting and describing fruits. (K1)
- Make a collection of pips. Investigate which pips grow into plants. (K2, 4)

Physical Development

- Tell a story in which children go fruit picking. Use benches as bridges, mats for strawberry fields and climbing apparatus for trees. Encourage children to pick fruit carefully and to move gracefully as they carefully carry their fruit. (PD1, 2, 7)
- Observe a range of fruit and vegetables before modelling ones with dough. Encourage children to mould the dough with their fingers and to pay attention to details such as stalks. (PD8)
  Note: Children with eczema or cuts on their hands should wear disposable gloves if working with salt dough.
- Cut fruit and vegetables from stiff, coloured card. Punch holes around the edge and encourage children to enjoy sewing/lacing activities. (PD8)

Creative Development

- Make papier maché fruit and vegetables by scrunching newsprint into the required shape, covering it with pieces of torn newsprint and watered down PVA glue and painting when firm and dry. (C3, 5)

- Enjoy printing with ready-mixed paints and hard vegetables and fruit. The prints are particularly effective on black sugar paper. If laminated they make excellent mats for giving as presents. (C3)
- Make caterpillar sock puppets by sticking eyes and feelers to socks that are no longer needed. Encourage children to enjoy using their puppets to tell the story of The Very Hungry Caterpillar. Provide materials for making props for the plays. (C1, 5)

Activity: The Very Hungry Caterpillar's Favourite Vegetables

Learning opportunity: Collaborating to make a big book. Early Learning Goal: Communication, Language and Literacy. Children should listen with enjoyment, and respond to stories. They should retell narratives in the correct sequence, drawing on language patterns of stories.

Resources: The Very Hungry Caterpillar by Eric Carle (Puffin); A3 sized stiff paper and punched, clear plastic wallets; crayons, pens and pencils; ribbon.

Key vocabulary: Names of vegetables and colours.

Organisation: Whole group.

What to do: Earlier in the week read The Very Hungry Caterpillar by Eric Carle (Puffin). Encourage children to notice all the fruits that appear in the book. Explain that later in the week the group is going to write a new story in which the caterpillar eats vegetables.

Later in the week, encourage children to retell the story by 'reading' the pictures. Begin the story again, but this time invite children to make suggestions for vegetables for the caterpillar to eat. Scribe the children's ideas and invite them to illustrate their ideas. Talk about the way the original story ends and talk about other ways to finish the book.

When all pages have been completed place them in A3 sized, punched plastic wallets and sew the pages together to make a sturdy big book for the group's library.

Activity: Eating grapes

Learning opportunity: Enjoying counting and using a number rhyme.

Early Learning Goal: Problem Solving, Reasoning and Numeracy. Children should say and use number names in order in familiar contexts.

Resources: A bunch of grapes made from ten purple or green circles of card fixed with Velcro onto a piece of stiff card.

Key vocabulary: Bunch, grape, numbers to ten.

Organisation: Whole group sitting comfortably on the floor.

What to do: Show children the bunch of grapes. Together count the grapes. Remove one grape and pretend to eat it. Ask children how many are left. Continue until all the grapes have been eaten. Replace the grapes and recite the eating grapes rhyme.

> Ten grapes in a bunch
> How many shall I have for lunch?
> One grape so sweet
> Leaving ... grapes for (child's name) to eat.

Within each verse invite a child to remove a grape. As children become more confident with the rhyme, vary the number of grapes that are eaten.

Display

Make a patchwork of the fruit and vegetable prints. Edge the patchwork with strips of border paper of a colour used within the prints. On a table in front arrange the papier maché and dough fruit and vegetables. Encourage children to make their own name labels.

Week 4
Food from around the world

Personal, Social and Emotional Development

- Invite adults known to the group to talk about their favourite food from around the world. Ask them to explain how the food is prepared. (PS1, 3)
- Make a display of food wrappers and pictures of food from different countries. Help children to make small flags to represent the countries from which the food came and add them to the display. (PS1, 6, 8)

Communication, Language and Literacy

- Make 'Thank you' cards for the parents who talk to the group about food from around the world. Help children to write simple messages and their own names. Encourage them to think of the sounds to begin and finish words. (L11, 18, 19)
- Encourage children to look closely at the words on the food wrappers from around the world and to sort them according to their initial sounds. (L9)
- Look through travel brochures for pictures of food. Provide children with books made from pieces of folded A3 sized paper. Encourage them to make their own travel brochures with pictures of exotic food. Use the brochures in a role-play travel agents (L9)

Problem Solving, Reasoning and Numeracy

- Use pasta for measuring lengths. Encourage children to use phrases such as 'longer than', 'shorter than', 'the same length as', 'longest' and 'shortest'. (N4)
- Make repeating pattern collages with pasta pieces. (N10)
- Make pizza jigsaws (see activity opposite). (N10)

Knowledge and Understanding of the World

- Observe bread from around the world. Encourage children to use magnifiers to compare the number of holes in pieces of different bread. Use ready-mixed paints to make prints of slices of bread. (K3) Note: Children who have coeliac disease must not eat bread that contains gluten.
- Use a globe to help children identify the countries from which different foods have come. (K2)

- Observe wet and dry tea bags (see activity opposite). (K1, 3)
- Begin to fill a scrap book with sticky labels from fruit and vegetables that show countries of origin. (K2)

Physical Development

- Show children how to use chopsticks to transfer beads or balls of tissue paper from one container to another. See how many can be moved before the sand in a minute timer runs out. (PD7)
- Use a range of balancing and climbing equipment for children to use as they go on an imaginary journey around the world. Encourage children to mime eating food special to a particular country such as rice in China, cheese in Holland and long pieces of spaghetti in Italy. (PD1, 2, 3, 4)

Creative Development

- Use pasta to make frames for a special picture. Stick pasta around the edge of a piece of card. When dry, adults can spray the frames gold or silver to give an antique effect. (C3)

- Use squared paper and pens/crayons to design new tartans for packaging shortbread from Scotland. (C3)
- Use string to make spaghetti patterns. Cover colourful paper plates with PVA glue and show children how to drop long pieces of string on to make spiralling, curly patterns. Varnish the patterns with watered down PVA glue. (C3)

Activity: Pizza jigsaws

Learning opportunity: Talking about patterns and shapes.

Early Learning Goal: Problem Solving, Reasoning and Numeracy. Children should talk about, recognise and recreate simple patterns.

Resources: Pizza sized circles of stiff card, small coloured regular shapes to represent cheese, tomatoes, pineapple chunks and so on.
Key vocabulary: Pizza, names of regular shapes, colours and pizza toppings.

Organisation: Small group.

What to do: Talk about pizzas. Explain that pizzas were first made in Italy. Describe favourite toppings. Show children the card circle that will be a pizza base and explain that together the group is going to make a pizza jigsaw. In turn invite children to select shapes, to say the foods that they represent and to stick them on to the pizza. Encourage the children to stick them so that each pizza piece would have the same topping. When complete, laminate the pizza or cover it with clear sticky-backed plastic. Cut it into six identical pieces. As a group remake the pizza.

Invite further groups to make two-, three-, four- and five-piece pizzas. Encourage children to enjoy playing with the jigsaws both in role-play food activities and for shape recognition and pattern describing tasks.

Activity: Observing tea bags

Learning opportunity: Observing using the senses of sight, touch, smell and hearing.

Early Learning Goal: Knowledge and Understanding of the World. Children should investigate objects and materials by using all of their senses as appropriate. They should look closely at similarities, differences and change.

Resources: Plastic magnifiers; tea bags; plastic beakers; warm water; plain paper; pencils; paper towel.

Key vocabulary: Tea bag, magnifier, same, different, change, country of origin for the tea.

Organisation: Small group.

What to do: Talk about the places where tea is grown. Talk about what tea is and how cups of tea can be made using tea bags. Show the group the tea bags. Invite the children to take it in turn to say something they notice about the tea bag. Encourage them to use magnifiers to notice the perforations, the fibres in the bag and the dusty tea. Ask them to smell the bag and to say what its scent reminds them of. Scribe the group's observations on a piece of card cut in the shape of the tea bag.

Place the bag in a cup of warm water. Encourage children to notice what happens to the bag and again scribe the observations. Finally, remove the bag from the water and compare it with a dry tea bag.

Display
Make a group collage of food packaging from around the world. Encourage children to collect as wide a range as possible. Involve children in sticking up their own packages and to think about where they can be best placed. Hang up the group's tea bag observations.

Week 5

Food from fairy tales and nursery rhymes

Personal, Social and Emotional Development

- Tell the story of 'Goldilocks and the Three Bears'. Talk about the porridge and why the bears had to wait for it to cool. Talk about Goldilocks' behaviour. (PS9)
- Enjoy listening to the story of 'Little Red Riding Hood'. As a group make a basket of food to take to Granny (see activity opposite). (PS5)

Communication, Language and Literacy

- Make a display of nursery rhyme and fairy tale books. Enjoy sharing the books. Encourage children to identify foods within the rhymes and stories. (L4)
- Make a big book of menus for fairy tale characters. Encourage children to imagine that they are a fairy tale character and to choose foods that are appropriate. Think about massive meals for the giant in 'Jack and the Beanstalk' and expensive meals for Prince Charming from the story of 'Cinderella'. (L4, 7, 18)
- Write new rhyming couplets for foods for Little Miss Muffet, for example 'Little Miss Muffet sat on a chair, eating a giant, purple pear'. (L4)

Problem Solving, Reasoning and Numeracy

- Use teddy bears, plastic bowls and cutlery and the story of 'Goldilocks and the Three Bears' for activities comparing, ordering and matching sizes. Create a role-play house for the three bears. (N9)

- Use 'Little Jack Horner' for number work (see activity opposite). (N5)
- Provide children with baskets cut from brown sugar paper for Little Red Riding Hood. Invite them to fill the baskets with foods cut from sticky paper and to count up how many of each kind of food is in the baskets. (N1, 2)

Knowledge and Understanding of the World

- Enjoy baking foods described within fairy tales and nursery rhymes. These could include gingerbread men (from 'The Gingerbread Man'), pancakes (from 'The Big Pancake'), porridge (from 'The Magic Porridge Pot' or 'Goldilocks and the Three Bears') or jam tarts (from 'The Queen of Hearts'). Encourage children to talk about and describe the ingredients and to notice the changes that take place when something is baked. Make sure to follow area safety guidelines for cooking activities. (K3)
- Use plain sponge cakes, icing and sweets to make houses as described in the story of 'Hansel and Gretel'. Encourage children to describe the things they use to make their houses. (K2)
(Most fairy tales can be found in the Ladybird Favourite Tales series.)

Physical Development

- Use the traditional story of The Enormous Turnip (Ladybird) to encourage children to move with imagination as they pretend to try and pick the giant turnip. (PD1)
- Use the traditional story of Jack and the Beanstalk (Ladybird) and climbing equipment to develop children's climbing skills. Encourage them to be Jack climbing the beanstalk in search of food. (PD1, 3)

Creative Development

- Involve children in painting portraits of fairy tale and nursery rhyme characters and the foods they like to eat. (C3)
- Make fairy tale and nursery rhyme stick puppets from pieces of card and lolly sticks. Enjoy using the puppets to act out nursery rhymes and to retell fairy tales. (C5)

- Enjoy singing 'When Goldilocks went to the house of the bears' from *Okki-tokki-unga Action Songs for Children* chosen by Beatrice Harrop, Linda Friend and David Gadsby (A & C Black). (C4)

Activity: Food for Little Red Riding Hood's Grandma

Learning opportunity: Thinking about feelings and needs.

Early Learning Goal: Personal, Social and Emotional Development. Children should have a developing awareness of their own needs, views and feelings, and be sensitive to the needs, views and feelings of others.

Resources: Pencils; crayons; postcard-sized pieces of card; large basket; book of 'Little Red Riding Hood'.

Key vocabulary: Names for foods in the basket.

Organisation: Whole group.

What to do: As a group enjoy sharing the tale of 'Little Red Riding Hood'. Encourage children to enjoy joining in with well-known phrases and to take it in turns to say what happens next. Talk about the kindness of Little Red Riding Hood in taking a basket of food for her Granny. Discuss why the Granny might have needed the food and what sort of foods would be good to have taken. Encourage children to give reasons for their suggestions. Invite children to draw their suggestions on the pieces of card and to place them in the basket for Granny.

Activity: Counting with Little Jack Horner

Learning opportunity: Adding and subtracting using numbers to five.

Early Learning Goal: Problem Solving, Reasoning and Numeracy. Children should, in practical activities and discussion, begin to use the vocabulary involved in adding and subtracting.

Resources: Plastic pudding basin with a lid; five table-tennis/airflow balls.

Key vocabulary: Plum, thumb, numbers to five.

Organisation: Whole group.

What to do: Together enjoy reciting the rhyme of 'Little Jack Horner'. Show the group the pudding basin and together count in two 'plums' for Jack. Take off the lid and remove one plum. Ask children how many plums are still in the basin. Continue to put in and take out plums, encouraging children to work out each time how many plums are still in the pie.

On further occasions recite the rhyme changing 'He pulled out a plum' to 'two', 'three', 'four' or 'five' plums. Encourage children to close their eyes and to make pictures in their heads of the basin with the plums.

Display

rhyme characters and food, leaving an outline of a thin black border. Display the characters on a large board around a checked piece of material or wallpaper as a picnic tablecloth. Place the food on the cloth. Make a label for the display to say 'Who will eat each food?' Encourage children to enjoy matching characters to likely food. Near the board place a book box of nursery rhyme and fairy tale books with the stick puppets.

Week 6
Food for special occasions

Personal, Social and Emotional Development
- Invite parents to come and talk about the food they prepare for special occasions. (PS13)
- Involve children in making plans for the 'Thank you for food' celebration. (PS8)

Communication, Language and Literacy
- Read a story that features a birthday, such as *Happy Birthday Blue Kangaroo* by Emma Chichester Clarke. Talk about birthday parties and children's favourite food. (L4)
- Look at recipe books. Help children to write recipes for special occasions (see activity opposite). (L5, 17)
- Together make up a new version of the song 'Here we go round the mulberry bush' to include actions for preparing food. The song could begin 'Here we go round the cooking pot' with lines such as 'This is the way we scrape the carrots' and 'This is the way we ice the cake'. Afterwards talk about the special occasions when the food might be eaten. (L4)

Problem Solving, Reasoning and Numeracy
- Provide children with pictures of birthday cakes with a number from one to nine written on each one. Encourage children to draw or stick on the corresponding number of candles. (N3)
- Ask each child to draw their favourite food for a special occasion. Use the pictures and large hoops for sorting and counting activities. (N1, 2, 6)
- Invite parents to work with groups of children to prepare foods that are special to their families. Encourage the parents to involve children in measuring the ingredients and comparing quantities. (N9)

Knowledge and Understanding of the World
- Invite parents and children to describe the foods that form part of special occasions celebrated within different cultures. Examples include Chinese New Year, Diwali, Passover and Christmas. (K2, 11)
- Talk about the table decorations used for meals to celebrate special occasions. Encourage children to design and make table decorations for a celebration. Cardboard tubes covered with shiny paper and tissue flames make effective model candles. (K2)
- Talk about the way crops are sown, grow and are harvested. As a group make a list of foods that are harvested. Talk about harvest celebrations as a time to give thanks for the people who grow the foods and also the foods themselves. (K9)

Physical Development
- Play the birthday cake game (see activity opposite). (PD2)
- Use playground chalk to draw pictures of food in a safe outside area. Encourage children to move in different ways as they visit each food. (PD1, 2, 4)

Creative Development
- Use clear plastic beakers and scrunched-up tissue paper to make new ice-cream sundaes/cocktails. Encourage children to talk about the colours of different flavoured ice creams/juices. Once in place the tissue paper can be varnished with a thin coat of watered down PVA glue. Provide straws/plastic spoons to add that finishing touch. (C3, 5)
- Enjoy singing 'Harvest' and 'Paint-box' from Harlequin 44 Songs Round the Year chosen by David Gadsby and Beatrice Harrop (A & C Black). (C4)
- On a large noticeboard make a wheelbarrow and a basket. Invite children to paint pictures of fruit, vegetables, bread and other foods for which they want to say 'Thank you'. Fill the barrow and basket with the children's paintings. (C4)
- Encourage children to enjoy making cakes and other meals for special occasions in the sand tray. (C5)

Activity: Recipes for special occasions

Learning opportunity: Writing for a purpose.

Early Learning Goal: Communication, Language and Literacy. Children should be able to extend their vocabulary,

exploring the meanings and sounds of new words. They should attempt writing for different purposes, using features of different forms such as... instructions.

Resources: A children's recipe book with clear pictures; A4 paper; a book of A4 sized, clear plastic wallets; crayons; pencils.

Key vocabulary: Recipe, names of foods, ingredients, mix, stir.

Organisation: Small group.

What to do: Encourage children to talk about times when they have baked. Talk about the ingredients and the things that children had to do. Show the group the recipe book. Together look at the pages. Read some of the instructions to the children and help them to notice the way instructions tend to be short and precise. Talk about foods that are eaten at special occasions and together write a new recipe. Allow children to use their imagination and don't worry if the ingredients don't go well together! When all recipes have been decorated, place them in the clear plastic wallets.

Activity: The birthday cake game

Learning opportunity: Moving with control.
Early Learning Goal: Physical Development. Children should move with control and coordination.

Resources: A chair; a large floor space; a tin decorated as a birthday cake.

Key vocabulary: Tiptoe, quietly, birthday cake.

Organisation: Whole group sitting on the floor in a circle.

What to do: The birthday cake game encourages children to develop both their fine and gross motor skills. Begin by showing the group the tin decorated as a birthday cake. Explain that it is a special cake and that children in turn will guard the cake. Invite a child to sit blindfolded on a chair in the middle of a circle of children seated on the floor. In turn point to children to try to tiptoe and take the cake. The guard stops the cake from being taken by pointing to where they hear a sound. Each guard is allowed to point three times before another one is chosen.

To make the game more difficult, place things inside the tin to make a noise.

Display

On a table put out safe bowls, jugs, cutlery and scales; the group's recipe book; empty packets of flour, sugar and so on for children to enjoy 'baking'. Nearby arrange the ice-cream sundaes and cocktails with a box of scrap materials for making more food for special occasions.

Bringing It All Together

The 'Thank you for food' celebration

Before starting the Food topic check with parents and carers that records concerning food allergies and special dietary needs are correct. Alert people who will be invited to the celebration of the date for the event.

Preparation

Explain to children that the purpose of the celebration is to say thank-you for food and to remember people who grow, make, sell and prepare food. Make a list of all the people who need to be remembered including those who package food and those who deliver it.

Involve children in making a food timeline by drawing pictures of each part of the process from the growing to the food appearing in a shop. Help children to appreciate the many people who are involved.

With the children plan and practise a small presentation in which they can show something that has been made during the topic, recite rhymes and sing songs. Allocate jobs so that all children have something special to do.

It may be appropriate for your group to use the celebration as a way to raise money for victims of famine. All children enjoy collecting money!

Food

Invite parents to provide finger foods that they have made at home with children. Encourage parents to think

about the weekly themes used within the topic and to prepare foods from the themes.

The celebration

Start the celebration with the presentation by the children. Ensure that items by individual children are balanced with ones by the whole group. Invite the audience to join in with the songs and actions.

Following the presentation ask people to remain seated whilst children, with adults to supervise, hand round the refreshments. To finish invite the guests to look around the displays and to join in a treasure hunt to find fruit cut from card hidden around the room. Make sure that enough fruits are hidden for everyone to find at least one.

Resources

Resources to collect

- For role-play cafes and shops - toy cash register, receipt book, plastic plates and cutlery, toy foods, menus.
- Green plastic counters.
- Large die numbered one to six.

Everyday resources

- Boxes, large and small for modelling.
- Papers and cards of different weights, colours and textures, for example sugar, corrugated card, silver and shiny papers and so on.
- Dry powder paints for mixing and mixed paints for covering large areas.
- Different sized paint brushes from household brushes to thin brushes for delicate work and a variety of paint mixing containers.
- A variety of drawing and colouring pencils, crayons, pastels, charcoals, and so on.
- Additional decorative and finishing materials such as sequins, foils, glitter, tinsel, shiny wool and threads, beads, pieces of textiles, parcel ribbon.
- Table covers
- Pasta
- Clean plastic bottles
- A3 sized, clear plastic, punched wallets

Stories

- *A Bear Called Paddington* by Michael Bond (Harper Collins).
- *The Very Hungry Caterpillar* by Eric Carle (Puffin).
- *Oliver's Fruit Salad* by Vivian French (Hodder Children's Books).
- *Happy Birthday Blue Kangaroo* by Emma Chichester Clarke (Harper Collins).
- *Oliver's Milkshake* by Vivian French (Hodder Children's Books).
- *Oliver's Vegetables* by Vivian French (Hodder Children's Books).
- *The Tiger Who Came to Tea* by Judith Kerr (Harper Collins).
- Fairytales from the Ladybird *Favourite Tales* collection:
    - The Gingerbread Man
    - Goldilocks and the Three Bears
    - The Magic Porridge Pot
    - Little Red Riding Hood
    - Hansel and Gretel
    - The Enormous Turnip
    - The Big Pancake

Songs

- *Harlequin 44 Songs Round the Year* chosen by David Gadsby and Beatrice Harrop (A & C Black).
- *Okki-tokki-unga Action Songs for Children* chosen by Beatrice Harrop, Linda Friend and David Gadsby (A & C Black).
- *Apusskido Songs for Children* chosen by Beatrice Harrop, Peggy Blakely and David Gadsby (A & C Black).

Poems

- *Out and About* by Shirley Hughes (Walker Books).
- *This Little Puffin* by Elizabeth Matterson (Puffin).
- *Pudding and Pie Favourite Nursery Rhymes* chosen by Sarah Williams (Oxford University Press).

Books for planning

- For more ideas on fruit: *Planning for Learning through Summer* by Rachel Sparks Linfield and Penny Coltman (Step Forward Publishing).
- For more ideas on vegetables: *Planning for Learning through Winter* by Rachel Sparks Linfield and Penny Coltman (Step Forward Publishing).
- For more ideas on healthy eating: *Healthy Eating* (Step Forward Publishing).
- *The Early Ywars Foundation Stage; Setting the Standards for Learning Development and Care for Children from Birth to Five* (Department for Children, Schools and Families).

Collecting Evidence of Children's Learning

Monitoring children's development is an important task. Keeping a record of children's achievements, interests and learning styles will help you to see progress and will draw attention to those who are having difficulties for some reason. If a child needs additional professional help, such as speech therapy, your records will provide valuable evidence.

Records should be the result of collaboration between group leaders, parents and carers. Parents should be made aware of your record keeping policies when their child joins your group. Show them the type of records you are keeping and make sure they understand that they have an opportunity to contribute. As a general rule, your records should form an open document. Any parent should have access to records relating to his or her child. Take regular opportunities to talk to parents about children's progress. If you have formal discussions regarding children about whom you have particular concerns, a dated record of the main points should be kept.

Keeping it manageable

Records should be helpful in informing group leaders, adult helpers and parents and always be for the benefit of the child. The golden rule is to make them simple, manageable and useful.

Observations will basically fall into three categories:
- **Spontaneous records:** Sometimes you will want to make a note of observations as they happen, for example, a child is heard counting cars accurately during a play activity, or is seen to play collaboratively for the first time.

- **Planned observations:** Sometimes you will plan to make observations of children's developing skills in their everyday activities. Using the learning opportunity identified for an activity will help you to make appropriate judgements about children's capabilities and to record them systematically.

To collect information:
- talk to children about their activities and listen to their responses;
- listen to children talking to each other;
- observe children's work such as early writing, drawings, paintings and 3D models. (Keeping photocopies or photographs can be useful.)

Sometimes you may wish to set up 'one off' activities for the purposes of monitoring development. Some pre-school groups, for example, ask children to make a drawing of themselves at the beginning of each term to record their progressing skills in both co-ordination and observation. Do not attempt to make records after every activity!

- **Reflective observations:** It is useful to spend regular time reflecting on the children's progress. Aim to make some brief comments about each child every week.

Informing your planning

Collecting evidence about children's progress is time consuming and it is important that it is useful. When you are planning, use the information you have collected to help you to decide what learning opportunities you need to provide next for children. For example, a child who has poor pencil or brush control will benefit from more play with dough or construction toys to build the strength of hand muscles.

Example of recording chart

Name: Libby Hardcastle		D.O.B. 31.3.03		Date of entry: 13.9.08	
Term	**Personal, Social and Emotional Development**	**Communication, Language and Literacy**	**Problem Solving, Reasoning and Numeracy**	**Knowledge and Understanding of the World**	**Physical Development**	**Creative Development**
ONE	Happy to say good-bye to mother. Engages with activities immediatly. 1.10.08 EMH	Enjoying listening to stories and reciting rhymes. Can write first name. Good with pencil grip. 13.10.08 EMH	Is able to say numbers to ten and count accurately five objects. Recognises and names squares and circles. 16.10.08 EH	Is eager to ask questions. Was fascinated by foods from around the world. 5.11.08 AC	Can balance on one leg. Loves useing climbing equipment. 9.11.08 AC	Made a wonderful pasta collage. Enjoys painting, mixing own colours. 29.9.08 LSS
TWO						
THREE						

Skills overview of six-week plan

Week	Topic Focus	Personal, Social and Emotional Development	Communication, Language and Literacy	Problem Solving, Reasoning and Numeracy	Knowledge and Understanding of the World	Physical Development	Creative Development
1	Favourite food	Listening; Expressing emotions; Sharing	Listening to stories; Writing; Recognising initial sounds	Recognising numerals; Recognising flat shapes; Counting	Counstructing; Talking	Aiming; Catching; Using malleable materials	Role-play; Collage; Painting
2	Buying and selling food	Listening; Taking turns; Saying please and thank-you	Role-play; Listening; Speaking; Writing	Counting; Recognising numerals; Comparing solid shapes; Using coins	Observing; Comparing; Describing; Investigating; Talking	Aiming; Using small equipment	Role-play; Sewing; Painting
3	Fruit and vegetables	Considering actions; Listening; Collaborating; Sharing	Listening and responding to stories; Speaking; Writing	Comparitive language; Counting; Measuring	Talking; Observing; Describing; Comparing	Moving with control and imagination; Using malleable materials	Papier maché; Printing; Making puppets and plays
4	Food from around the world	Sensitivity to others; Speaking; Listening	Recognising initial and final sounds; Writing; Role-play	Comparitive language; Making and recognising patterns	Talking; Observing; Comparing; Identifying	Moving with control and imagination; Using small equipment	Using materials; Exploring colours
5	Food from fairy tales and nursery rhymes	Sensitivity to others; Awarness of what is right and wrong	Listening to stories and rhymes; Repsonding to stories and rhymes; Writing	Counting; Using the languageof addition and subtraction; Comparing	Investigating; Observing; Talking	Moving with control and imagination; Climbing	Singing; Painting; Using materials; Making and using puppets
6	Food for special occasions	Sensitivity to others; Collaborative planning	Listening to stories and songs; Writing; Making up a song	Recognising numerals; Counting; Comparing quantities	Talking; Awarness of special occasions within cultures	Moving imagination, control and awarness of space	Painting; Using material; Singing

Home links

The theme of Food lends itself to useful links with children's homes and families. Through working together children and adults gain respect for each other and build comfortable and confident relationships.

Establishing partnerships
● Keep parents informed about the topic of Food and the themes for each week. By understanding the work of the group, parents will enjoy the involvement of contributing ideas, time and resources.
● Photocopy the parent's page for each child to take home.
● Invite friends, childminders and families to share all or part of the 'Thank-you for food' celebration.

Visiting enthusiasts
● Invite adults to come to the group to talk about food from around the world.
● Invite shopkeepers, farmers, bakers, people who work in cafes and those who deliver food to come and talk about their work with food.

Resource requests
● Ask parents to contribute clean packaging from food for modelling, sorting and role-play activities.
● Show parents how to undo cereal packets and remake them inside out. Enlist their help in producing clean boxes for model making.
● Ask parents to save mail order catalogues, travel brochures and colour supplement magazines. They are invaluable for a range of cutting, making and sorting activities.

The 'Thank you for food' celebration
● It is always useful to have extra adults at times such as the celebration event. Involve parents in preparing refreshments and in helping children to participate.